Contents

Introduction

- **A**diaphoron 1
- **B**ells 2
- **C**hancel 4
- **D**ecoration 5
- **E**levation 7
- **F**ish 8
- **G**ottesdienst 10
- **H**ymnal 11
- **I**nvocation 12
- **J**esus 13
- **K**eys 16
- **L**ord's Supper 17
- **M**odes of Baptism 19
- **N**ew Testament 20
- **O**rder 22
- **P**entecost 23
- **Q**uadragesima 25
- **R**eformation 26
- **S**unday 27
- **T**radition 28
- **Eu**logy 29
- **V**ows 30
- **W**eddings 31
- **(X)** Your Name 32
- **Y**our Role in Worship 33
- **(Z)** Omega 34

Introduction

The Lutheran church is the only church that teaches exactly what the Bible says, no more and no less. Many churches make that claim, but they add human traditions or human logic or human feeling to their teachings. The Lutheran church uses the Bible the way God says he wants us to use it, with Jesus as the focal point of every word: "You diligently study the Scriptures because you think that by them you possess eternal life. These are the Scriptures that testify about me" (Jesus speaking in John 5:39).

While Lutherans claim to teach exactly what the Bible says, they also observe many human traditions and customs in their worship that are not commanded by God. Is this a contradiction? Not at all! Lutherans make a clear distinction between what God's Word commands and human traditions, which we are free to follow or not.

This little primer is intended to help you understand better what it means to be Lutheran. Letter by letter, point by point, you will see how the Lutheran church teaches only the Bible. You will also see how the Lutheran church treasures worship traditions that glorify Jesus, the focal point of every word of the Bible. As you study what the Bible says, the Holy Spirit will give you a deeper appreciation of the gospel, the good news of forgiveness and salvation through faith in Jesus Christ. And you will see how that deep appreciation of the gospel is reflected in the way that Lutherans worship. It's as easy as ABC.

adiaphoron

Adiaphoron (ah-dee-AH-four-on; plural: adiaphora) is not a word you run across very often, but it's something important to help you understand what it means to be Lutheran. An adiaphoron is something neither commanded nor forbidden in God's Word. An adiaphoron is something God's Word has no direct comment on; God does not say it is right or wrong, that we have to do it or that we cannot do it.

How we design and decorate our church buildings is an adiaphoron. How we structure the way we worship is an adiaphoron. The times and seasons of our worship—these are adiaphora. Even the special services we have and our individual roles in them are all adiaphora.

Lutherans do not look at adiaphora and ask, "How much can we get away with?" The Bible has some advice about that attitude: "You, my brothers, were called to be free. But do not use your freedom to indulge the sinful nature; rather, serve one another in love" (Galatians 5:13).

Lutherans believe that the best approach to adiaphora is to ask, "What's the best way to demonstrate the love of Jesus Christ in these activities?" We study church history and see which worship forms have worked across cultures and across time to demonstrate the love of Jesus. We also see which practices have led to abuses and false doctrine in the church. Using the Bible, we evaluate what people before us have done, keeping the good and eliminating the bad. The Bible gives us the principles we need to improve our worship so that the gospel continues to be clearly presented there.

As we make choices for worship, both individually and as a group, we keep in mind 1 Corinthians 10:31: "Whether you eat or drink or whatever you do, do it all for the glory of God."

When we look at adiaphora with that attitude, we are teaching and living exactly what the Bible says, even when we are teaching and doing things the Bible does not speak about directly.

bells

Many Lutheran church services begin with the tolling of a bell. Where did that practice come from?

The Bible does not mention the large bells that churches ring. The Old Testament mentions some smaller bells worn by people and animals, but that's it.

Historians trace the ringing of bells for church services back to the 800s. At that time Christianity was spreading through northern Europe, and the Italian and Greek missionaries needed a way to tell the pagan German and English tribes when it was time to come to church. There were no radios or TVs or even newspapers. People did not wear watches. The missionaries decided that the best way to tell people when to come to church was to ring a big bell. The unique sound would be heard throughout the countryside, and the people would realize that it was time to come to worship. People who loved Jesus were thrilled when the bells rang, because that meant it was time to come worship him again.

Bells were soon used to announce special news, such as births and deaths. Around 1800, inventors designed mechanical systems of bells to play melodies. These bell systems became known as carillons. When they play the melodies of songs that praise Jesus, they invite people to remember the gospel. Today both mechanical and electronic sounds call people to worship.

People who built churches and wanted a good place to hang the bells made special high points called steeples. They chose the highest places in the area to build the churches, and the steeples were the highest points on the church. Consequently, the steeples could generally be seen for miles around. People imagined that they pointed to heaven. Since the gospel of Jesus does point us to heaven, many Lutheran churches include steeples as part of their building.

At the top of many steeples you will see a cross. The cross is probably the most common Christian symbol—even people who are not Christian recognize the crosses that decorate Lutheran churches. Why a cross? Because "we preach Christ crucified" (1 Corinthians 1:23), that is, Christ dying on a cross to take the punishment for our sins and win heaven for us. When Jesus rose from the dead, he made his death the most important event in all of human history.

There are other important events in history, of course, and the names of our churches celebrate some of them. Sometimes Lutheran churches are named after famous Christians, and when we say the names of those churches, we remember how they showed their faith in Jesus. Lutheran churches are also named after events in the life of Jesus, names of Jesus, or fruits of faith that the Holy Spirit works in our hearts.

The name Lutheran was actually given to our church by its enemies. They were trying to emphasize that it was founded by a mere man (the German, Martin Luther), not by the God-man, Jesus Christ. But Lutherans took the name proudly, because they knew that to be Lutheran was to found everything on the God-man, Jesus Christ. Many Lutherans added the name Evangelical to their churches, meaning that it teaches the gospel.

People who have never been inside a Lutheran church have heard the bells and seen the steeples, observed the crosses and read the names. Each of those things give a little taste of the gospel, but the real meal is inside.

chancel

Walk into a Lutheran church. Sometimes the doors will lead you into a hallway or into a small room, but more often you will enter an area where people gather outside of the worship space. That area is called the *narthex* (from a Greek word that means "narrow").

Now look into the place where people worship. If the church has a traditional design, the whole building will have a floor plan in the shape of a cross. The longer part, where people sit, is called the *nave* (from a Latin word that means "ship"). If the church has a more modern design, there will be more than one aisle, so there will be more places for people to sit closer to the front. Some churches provide large benches called *pews* (an Old English word for bench) for people to sit in.

No matter how the church is designed, the focal point will be in front. The lighting, the colors, and the arrangement of the seats will all draw your eyes to one place: the *chancel* (from a Latin word that means "railing," referring to the place in many churches where people gather to take the Lord's Supper). The chancel is the space in the front of the church with special decorations and special furniture. The chancel is the place where special things happen.

One of the special pieces of chancel furniture in your Lutheran church is probably the baptismal *font* (from a Latin word that means "fountain"). When it is used, the only true God adopts people into his family and gives them his name. They receive forgiveness of sins, life, and salvation.

Another special piece of chancel furniture in your Lutheran church is the *altar* (from a Latin word that means "a raised place"). When it is used, gifts of prayer and praise are lifted up before God, and his gifts of forgiveness are distributed to us in the Lord's Supper.

In some Lutheran churches there is a special piece of furniture from which the pastor preaches, called a *pulpit* (from a Latin word that means "stage"). When it is used, the Word of God is spoken to create and strengthen faith in Jesus. In churches where it is raised up, there is often a smaller lectern (a place for reading) from which the Scriptures are read before the sermon. Some churches have kept both places, even when the pulpit and lectern are on the same level, while some have only one place from which the Word of God is spoken.

The Bible does not instruct us to have any of these special pieces of furniture. But it does tell us to honor the Word of God and to administer God's sacraments faithfully. Lutheran churches use special furniture to make the chancel of the church a special place in order to give God's Word and sacraments the highest priority in the building. God's Word and sacraments are the way that God gives us his grace.

decoration

Look around a Lutheran church. What do you see? Lutheran churches that are designed well use decorative lighting to draw your eyes to the front of the church. The chancel is the brightest part, because that's where the most important things happen. That's where the Word of God is spoken and the sacraments are administered.

In addition to bright, modern lights, you will probably see candles in the front of the church. Before electricity, they were the best way to light up a chancel. But they are more than *decoration*. In the Bible, fire reminded people of the presence of the Holy Spirit in worship. The oil that is burned in some candles today reminds us of how the Holy Spirit had the Old Testament people use oil to anoint prophets, priests, and kings. That same oil also reminds us of how the Holy Spirit anointed Jesus to be the great Prophet, Priest, and King. Finally, the flame of the candle reminds us of how the Holy Spirit came on Jesus' disciples at Pentecost and made them reliable when they wrote down the Word of God for us in the Bible.

    That same flame reminds us that Jesus himself is the Light of the world. Many Lutheran churches have two candles on the altar as a reminder that Jesus is both human and divine. Some Lutheran churches light those candles only when celebrating the Lord's Supper.

    In the front of a Lutheran church you will not see just light. You will also see color, lots of it. Sometimes that color will be in beautiful stained glass windows that show various scenes from the Bible. Sometimes it will be in brightly colored pieces of cloth, called *paraments* (from a Latin word that means "ornament"), that have Christian words or symbols on them. Sometimes the color will be on the clothing that the pastor wears to draw your attention away from him and onto God. All of the color is supposed to make you think of certain messages from the Bible.

    Black is the color for death, the result of sin. White is the color for holiness, the righteousness of God given to us through faith in Jesus. Red is the color for the blood of Jesus, which cleanses us from all sin, and for the Holy Spirit's fire. Purple is the color of the robe Jesus wore when he suffered. Green is the color for a faith that is growing in the pure Word of God. Blue is the color for the hopeful anticipation we feel as we look to the sky for Jesus to come again.

    Many Lutheran churches also have flowers in the front of church. The colors of the flowers are less important than the idea that growing things produce beautiful results. When people are growing in faith, they produce beautiful good works.

    Lutheran churches often have other pieces of art in their churches. The Bible does not tell us what art to have there. But with our decorations, we are carrying out the words of the Bible when it says, "Whatever is true, whatever is noble, whatever is right, whatever is pure, whatever is lovely, whatever is admirable—if anything is excellent or praiseworthy—think about such things" (Philippians 4:8).

elevation

Most Lutheran churches have ceilings higher than you find in an average home. By making the space where we worship a little bit different from the space where we do normal, everyday things, we are trying to give a sense of the awe we feel in the presence of God. God is present everywhere, but he is present in a special way when we worship. He comes to us in a special way in the sacraments; he speaks directly to us in his Word. We give *elevated* attention to these things, so we elevate the roof of the building where we find them.

Most Lutheran churches also elevate various symbols, particularly the cross. The cross on which Jesus died was on a mountain, and if we lift up our eyes to that particular hill, we sense that something special is going on. Here we see a person who did not deserve to die but died anyway, in the place of others. We lift up our eyes to see perfect love in action. Some day we will lift up our eyes again when we see Jesus return, elevated and glorified.

Some Lutheran churches have an empty cross in the front of the church to remind us that Jesus is no longer crucified. Rather, he is risen from the dead. Others have a cross with a representation of Jesus' body on it (called a crucifix) to remind us that Jesus was a real human being who suffered a real death.

Some Lutheran churches elevate the bread and wine when the words of institution are spoken to show that we are celebrating the Lord's Supper. Most Lutheran pastors elevate their hands when they use the Word of God to bless the people who have come to worship. A few Lutheran churches even elevate the Bible when it is being read.

What you may have noticed about Lutheran worship is that the people even elevate themselves. There are times when they stand and when they sit. At some Lutheran churches there are even times when they kneel. The kneeling shows humility; the standing shows respect. Lutherans stand during worship—whether singing, praying, or listening—when they want to indicate their respect for God and his Word. There is a custom of rising when someone important enters the room or is about to speak—and no one is more important than our Savior. He's got something important to say to us.

fish

Why are there sometimes *fish* symbols in Lutheran churches? And how about those letters that don't seem to spell any recognizable words? Lutheran churches use symbols that extend all the way back to the time when Jesus walked the earth. When you find out what they mean, they remind you of precious biblical truths.

The fish symbol is one of the most interesting. The Greek word for fish is *IXTHUS*. Each letter of that word is the first letter of the Greek words for "Jesus Christ, God's Son, Savior," so the Greek word for fish is an acrostic. It's used as a confession of faith.

Here are the meanings for some other symbols:

Alpha-Omega: The first and last letters of the Greek alphabet. Jesus is called the Alpha and Omega in the Bible

(Revelation 1:8; 21:6; 22:13). Jesus has existed for all eternity and will continue to exist to all eternity.

Butterfly: Symbol for the resurrection of the dead. Although a caterpillar does not die when it goes into its cocoon, it does look a lot different when it comes out! Although our bodies will still be our bodies when we rise from the dead, we will be a lot different because the effects of sin will be gone entirely.

Chi-Rho: The X (chi) is the first letter of the Greek word for Christ. The P (rho) is the second letter.

Chi-Sigma: The X (chi) is the first letter of the Greek word for Christ. The C (sigma) is the last letter.

Crown: Reminds us that Jesus is the King of kings and Lord of lords.

Crown of thorns: Was placed on the Savior's head before the crucifixion and reminds us of our Lord's Passion.

Grapes and a sheaf of wheat: Reminds us of the earthly elements in the Lord's Supper.

IHC or IHS: The first three letters of the Greek word for Jesus.

INRI: The first letters of the Latin words for "Jesus (of) Nazareth, King (of the) Jews." This is what the Roman governor Pilate had written on the cross.

Iota-Chi: The I (iota) is the first letter of the Greek word for Jesus. The X (chi) is the first letter of the Greek word for Christ.

Iota-Sigma: The I (iota) is the first letter of the Greek word for Jesus. The S (sigma) is the last letter of that same word.

NIKA or NIKE: The Greek word for victory. With Jesus' resurrection, death has been swallowed up in victory.

Palm branch: To remind us how Jesus was praised as he entered Jerusalem on Palm Sunday.

Shell: The shell, with three drops of water, reminds us of the water used in Baptism.

Triangle, triangle in a circle, or triangle with three-leaf clover or three circles: Symbols for our God, who is three divine persons, but one God.

There are also many different cross symbols. Most churches use a traditional Roman cross, and it's likely, but not absolutely certain, that the cross on which Jesus was crucified had that shape. But the shape is not important. More important is that people who see a cross know and trust that Jesus won forgiveness for them when he died on it.

G
gottesdienst

Gottesdienst is a German word that means "service of God." It's the word that German-speaking people use to describe their church service. It's a very fitting word for worship, because it means both "God's service to us" and "our service to God."

Most Lutherans worship using a standard format called a *liturgy* (from a Greek word that means "service"). In some parts of the liturgy, God serves us with his Word and sacraments. In other parts, we serve him with our prayers and praise.

The next time you are in church, pay attention to each part of the service. See whether it is God serving us with the gospel or our response to that gospel in word or song. You will notice that the rhythm of the service is God giving us his Word followed by our response of prayer or praise. Notice also that there is more coming from God than there is going to God. The emphasis is on God, not on us.

That emphasis on God's gospel coming to us is one way to identify good Lutheran worship. If there is a lot coming from the people but not much coming from God, the emphasis shifts to the human part of worship, and we miss out on the better, divine things. But if the majority of time and effort is spent on what God says to us, the emphasis is just where it belongs.

Most Lutheran churches tell you in a little folder called a

bulletin which Scripture readings are being read and which hymns are being sung. Often an adult volunteer, called an usher, distributes the bulletins and can help you find a seat.

hymnal

That big book that Lutherans have in church with the songs printed in it—that's called a *hymnal*. The songs inside are called hymns (from a Greek word that means "song in praise of God"). The book also contains the liturgies, usually in the pages just before the hymns.

How were the hymns chosen to be in the hymnal? Well, to be honest, there was usually just a committee or an individual that made the choices. But why did they choose the songs they did and decide they are fit for the hymnal?

Fortunately, some committees have put into writing what they looked for in a song for a hymnal. The committee that chose the hymns for *Christian Worship: A Lutheran Hymnal* (CW) listed a few qualities of a good hymn: liturgical, doxological (from a Greek word that means "bringing glory to God"), makes use of the Word of God, poetic, has emotional content, is influenced by the "year of our Lord," and has a melody that supports the scriptural message and touches the heart of the worshiper.

The CW committee also wrote, "A good hymn has doctrinal content. If the praise of God speaks of the great things God has done, this will almost always appear in a form that teaches. The chief doctrine Christian hymnody should proclaim is mankind's redemption from sin through Jesus Christ, Lord and Savior" (*Christian Worship: Manual*, page 231).

Good hymns come in all kinds of musical styles, and they

can be accompanied by all kinds of musical instruments. There are no specific rules about musical styles and instruments in the Bible. Most Lutheran churches accompany hymns with an organ, because that instrument is one of the best for supporting the singing of large groups. Lutheran churches strive to use musical styles and instruments that help worshipers focus their thoughts on the message of God's Word.

Many Lutheran churches form choirs to practice music ahead of time and help the congregation with it. The custom of having a choir dates all the way back to the Old Testament. The Bible describes the elaborate musical preparations for worship in the temple in Jerusalem (1 Chronicles 15,16). A choir of angels sang at the birth of Jesus. The book of Revelation describes the choirs of believers in heaven. A good church choir can give you a little musical taste of the joy that goes along with those events.

Most Lutheran hymnals have other useful parts: special arrangements of the Bible's psalms, prayers for individuals and groups, and charts to help in worship. Look through your hymnal the next time you are in church. If you have not already thought of it, consider buying your own hymnal and using it in worship, both in church and at home.

I
invocation

Have you ever noticed that most Lutheran services start the same way? Either the pastor mentions the "name of the Father and of the Son and of the Holy Spirit" or the congregation sings a hymn that mentions the names of the persons of the Trinity.

Lutherans call that way of beginning the service the *invocation* (from a Latin word that means "call on"). We call on the name of the Lord to show that the service is for worshiping the only true God, the one God who has revealed himself as three divine persons: Father, Son, and Holy Spirit. We call on the true God to bless us in our worship. We call on God with every person in worship hearing us to recognize that we gather only to praise the true God, not for any other reason.

There are different liturgies that come after the invocation. The most common liturgy is called the Common Service. Its roots go back to Old Testament worship, and it is found in its present basic form over 1,500 years ago. Millions of believers over many generations have used it as a way to honor God by listening to his Word.

Another liturgy is called the Service of Word and Sacrament. It uses other historical forms of worship that have proven themselves as very good ways to communicate the gospel. A shorter version, the Service of the Word, has less music but keeps the same number of Bible readings. In this service there is no celebration of the Lord's Supper.

There are also special services for certain times of day, such as Morning Praise and Evening Prayer. These services recognize that the gospel gives us the freedom to choose when and how we gather for worship.

Of course, the gospel gives us the freedom to have any form of worship that glorifies God rather than human beings. When we start with the invocation, we have started exactly that way.

Jesus

It is important to see how each part of the liturgy up until the sermon points to *Jesus*.

Confession of Sins: After the invocation, most Lutheran

liturgies include a confession spoken by the congregation. Since Lutherans believe that Christians may go directly to God for forgiveness, we confess our sins in public. Doing that at the beginning of the service helps us to remember the sinful condition in which we come to worship, and it reminds us that no one is better than another. It focuses our attention on our need for Jesus. Some Lutheran pastors step out of the chancel for this part of the service, physically joining the congregation as a fellow sinner.

Kyrie ("Lord, Have Mercy"): In both the Old and New Testament, believers prayed in worship. The kyrie was the Christian response after each part of the prayer was spoken by the worship leader. After a certain number of individual requests, each with the congregation responding, "Lord, have mercy on us" (*Kyrie, eleison* in Greek), the congregation ended the prayer by singing the phrase three times in a row. We pray for God's mercy in view of what Jesus has done for us.

Absolution (from a Latin word that means "acquittal"): Lutherans teach that your sins are forgiven with no strings attached. You are declared not guilty, or acquitted, of your sin because Jesus has taken the punishment for it. Therefore, in a Lutheran church you hear your forgiveness spoken in public. Lutheran pastors who have stepped out of the chancel to confess their sins now step back into the chancel to speak as God's representative.

Gloria in Excelsis Deo (Latin for "Glory be to God in the Highest"): This long hymn verse is one example of a canticle, a song from the Bible other than one from the book of psalms. The canticles date from the earliest Christian times. The angels sang the first words of this canticle when Jesus was born. In *Christian Worship* it is used to express our joy because we are forgiven.

Salutation: When the worship leader says, "The Lord be with you" and the congregation answers, "And also with you," it is the ancient way of saying "good morning." In *Christian Worship* it is put with the Collect to show that pastor and people are really praying for one another with these words. This kind of Christian friendship, bringing together people of different sexes and ages and cultures, is only possible because of the love of Jesus.

Prayer of the Day: The prayer of the day is called a proper, a part of the service that changes every week. The prayers we use at this point in worship have a recognizable form: (1) address to God the Father, (2) reference to a characteristic of God, (3) actual petition, and (4) concluding praise mentioning the Trinity, sometimes including a reason for the petition. The work of Jesus is what makes it possible for us to approach God in prayer.

The Prayer of the Day is the last part of the service in which *we come to God*. Following the prayer, *God comes to us* for the rest of the service, and we respond. That is why the pastor generally moves at this point from the altar to the lectern or pulpit.

First Lesson: In this reading, often from the Old Testament, we see how God revealed that Jesus the Savior was coming thousands of years before he actually came. During the Easter season, this reading comes from the New Testament book of Acts and shows us how the good news about Jesus went out to the world after his resurrection.

Psalm and Gloria Patri (Latin for "Glory be to the Father"): The psalms are the songs of praise of the Old Testament. We sing a psalm at this point in the service to express our response to the news of the coming Savior. The earliest Christians added the name of the Trinity to the end of every psalm to show that they were living in the New Testament after the arrival of Jesus on the earth. We continue that practice since we are still living in the New Testament era.

Second Lesson (*Epistle*, the Greek word for "letter"): This is a reading from a New Testament letter, chosen especially to highlight some word or work of Jesus. It often includes an encouragement to live a Christian life of faith.

Verse of the Day: Dating back all the way to biblical

times, these verses are either said or chanted as a way to prepare ourselves for the most important reading of the service: a reading from one of the four gospels, where the life of Jesus is recorded. We respond to hearing the Word of God in the traditional Old Testament way, with the word *Alleluia* (Hebrew for "Praise to the Lord").

Gospel: This is a reading from one of the four New Testament gospels, all of which tell about the life of Jesus. We often stand for the reading, not because we are coming to God (the reason for standing in the early part of the service) but out of respect. For the same reason, we often precede and follow it with short shouts of praise.

Creed (from a Latin word that means "believe"): We confess the faith in Jesus as our Savior that the Holy Spirit has strengthened through the readings.

Hymn of the Day: The song before the sermon is often a poetic setting of the words from Bible that are the basis for the sermon. It sets the tone for the sermon and focuses us, through music, on Jesus.

Sermon: The ideal sermon gives us a better understanding of how the Bible readings for the day point to Jesus. It also suggests applications to our lives. Already in the Old Testament, the worship leaders had the custom of commenting on the readings; Jesus himself did that at the synagogue in Nazareth (Luke 4:16-21). Sometimes those comments are called a homily, especially when they are brief and based on only one text.

keys

What are *keys* good for? When it finally comes right down to it, they're only good for locking or unlocking things.

Lutherans talk about the keys that Jesus has given to every

believer, the keys to lock or unlock heaven. The use of the keys is the special power and right that Christ gave to his church on earth: to forgive the sins of penitent sinners, but to refuse forgiveness to the impenitent as long as they do not repent.

When Jesus first told his disciples, "If you forgive anyone his sins, they are forgiven; if you do not forgive them, they are not forgiven" (John 20:23), they recognized the awesome individual responsibility they had. They forgave one another as penitent sinners in private and in public.

After a few hundred years, however, some people said that only ministers in the church could really forgive you. People neglected to forgive one another in public and in private. The result was more and more impenitence. People also looked for forgiveness in their own good works or in special religious items.

The Lutheran Reformation emphasized the power of the keys that every member of the church already holds. Lutherans put a confession of sins and public forgiveness into worship, right at the beginning. The gospel of Jesus Christ became the most important thing in worship again.

When a Christian forgives another Christian, it is as if Christ himself is speaking the forgiveness. Many still recognize the Lutheran church as the only Christian church that teaches forgiveness of sins through the work of Jesus without any strings attached.

L
Lord's Supper

It is important to see how each part of the liturgy, from the sermon through the end of the service when we celebrate the *Lord's Supper*, points to Jesus. But since the Bible does not say that we have to celebrate the Lord's Supper at every service, sometimes we go directly from the prayers to the benediction.

Offering: We offer money for the work of teaching about Jesus at our local congregation and in missions around the world.

Prayers: In the name of Jesus, we adore our Lord for his greatness, confess our unworthiness, thank God for specific blessings, and ask him for continued gifts.

The Lord's Prayer: We pray this excellent model prayer that came from the lips of the Savior when his disciples asked him how they should pray.

Preface: These sentences are among the oldest parts of the Christian liturgy. They set up the prayers of thanksgiving that have preceded the Lord's Supper ever since Jesus instituted it. They always focus on the work of Jesus.

Sometimes the Lord's Supper is called the Eucharist (from a Greek word that means "give thanks") to emphasize these prayers of thanksgiving.

Holy, Holy, Holy (*Sanctus*, the Latin word for "holy"): The great hymn of praise in the Communion service, the Sanctus connects Isaiah's vision of heaven (Isaiah 6) with Jesus' entry into Jerusalem (Matthew 21).

Words of Institution: These are the words Jesus spoke when he instituted the Lord's Supper.

The Distribution: In the early church, ministers distributing the bread and wine said simply, "The body of Christ" and "The blood of Christ." Lutherans say these or similar words so that no one is confused about what is being received with the bread and wine. Sometimes the Lord's Supper is called Holy Communion to emphasize that when we eat the bread and drink the wine, we are participating in the true body and blood of the Savior (1 Corinthians 10:16).

Usually the congregation sings the "Agnus Dei" (Latin for "Lamb of God") before or during the distribution. The song recalls that Jesus is the Lamb of God, who takes away the sin of the world. Some Lutherans sing hymns about the Lord's Supper while it is being distributed.

Since the Bible does not tell us the exact form of the bread and wine, some Lutheran congregations distribute the bread from a large loaf. Most use smaller pieces of bread called wafers. Some Lutheran congregations also use one large cup (chalice) for the wine, while others use smaller individual cups.

Closing Prayers: We offer a prayer of thanksgiving after the Lord's Supper, either "Thank the Lord" or the "Nunc Dimittis" (Latin for "Now you let depart"), another canticle. The "Nunc Dimittis" is the song that Simeon sang after seeing Jesus for the first time (Luke 2:28-32).

The Benediction (from a Latin word that means "good word"): Both Old Testament and New Testament words are used to bless people who have heard the gospel of Jesus and celebrated its power in their lives.

modes of Baptism

The Bible requires only two things for Baptism: water and the Word of God. The Word is specifically spoken by Jesus: "In the name of the Father and of the Son and of the Holy Spirit" (Matthew 28:19). The water comes from the Greek word *baptize*, which means "wash with water." It does not mean "immerse," although the word does not rule out baptizing that way.

The Bible does not tell us the *mode of Baptism*, that is, how much water to use or how to put it on a person. The first generation of Christians after Jesus' disciples described their custom in a document we call *The Didache*: "Baptize in running water in the name of the Father and of the Son and of the Holy Spirit. If you do not have running water, baptize in some other. If you cannot in cold, then in warm. If you have neither, pour water on the head three times."

The Bible also does not tell us the age of people to be baptized. He commands us to baptize "all nations" (Matthew

28:19) and says that the promises of Baptism are for both adults and children (Acts 2:39). God does not exclude anyone from Baptism because of age or sex or race. Baptism links us to Jesus, clothing us with Christ (Galatians 3:27) and connecting us to Christ's resurrection (1 Peter 3:21).

Some Lutheran churches place their baptismal font at the entrance of the church to show that Baptism is the way we become believers in Christ and enter into the church of Christ. Most Lutheran churches baptize both adults and children as part of the service, since it reminds Christians of their own baptism. It also reminds the congregation to pray for its newest members.

N
New Testament

The people who first received the gospels and letters of the *New Testament*—what did they do in their church services?

The earliest Christians were mostly Jewish, so it was natural for them to worship the way they always had in their synagogue. As a result, the oldest parts of our service are Jewish and date back to the Old Testament.

Old Testament believers read or chanted the psalms in a three-year cycle, which New Testament believers continued. Sometimes they read the psalms as lessons, used them as subjects for sermons, or sang them at different points in the service. Bible passages other than psalms were also read or sung responsively (one line by one group and the next line by another group, back and forth), preserved today as short sentences read or sung responsively by the pastor and the congregation. Whenever we sing or say "Alleluia" in the service, we are imitating Old Testament Jewish believers.

After a couple hundred years of reading and studying the New Testament, believers began expanding the Jewish forms and adding ideas with local flavor. Since the New Testament was read in the services, church leaders organized series of readings, called *pericopes* (from a Greek word that means "section"), that varied from place to place. Worship forms were expanding and God's people were joyfully singing new songs.

About the year 600, Gregory, the bishop of Rome, decided to make the service more uniform among the churches. After looking at a number of regional forms, he seems to have chosen the most common worship service in southern France (the "Gallic Rite"). Making a number of modifications, he announced one liturgy for the church, one pericope system, and one language: Latin. His choice for the musical system of the liturgy became known as Gregorian chant. Since very few people in the farthest parts of the empire knew Latin, Gregory suggested that the choir be trained to sing the responses in the liturgy while the congregation simply listened. This suggestion deadened congregational participation so much that it was an innovation for Lutheran congregations at the time of the Reformation to sing hymns during the service.

Some early New Testament practices, however, were preserved in the liturgy. One thing that remained was the last word of the Bible's last book: *Amen*, a Hebrew word for agreeing that something is true. In his description of Christian worship in the middle of the second century, a man commonly referred to as Justin Martyr tells us that prayers always concluded with a vigorous "amen" by the congregation. Justin says, "They shouted in applause."

Today we still use the Hebrew *amen* to say that we agree with what was spoken or sung. Every time we gather for worship, we join the four living creatures in Revelation who said "Amen!" and the elders who fell down and worshiped.

order

The key truth of the Christian faith is the gospel: "All have sinned and fall short of the glory of God, and are justified freely by his grace through the redemption that came by Christ Jesus" (Romans 3:23,24). The gospel frees us from the consequences of sin, takes away our guilt, and releases us from death.

The gospel also causes a spontaneous outpouring of gratitude and praise, of love and respect for God. The Bible calls this thankful response worship. This worship takes place throughout our lives, at home or at school or at work or at play (Romans 12:1). Christians are free to express their thanks to God in all kinds of ways.

Every God-pleasing thought, word, and action that a Christian does from a heart of faith is worship, but the highest worship of God is to listen as he speaks to us. In Luke 10:38-42 we see a woman who expressed her faith by being busy and another woman who expressed her faith by listening to Jesus. Jesus commends the one who is listening. After all, "Faith comes from hearing the message, and the message is heard through the word of Christ" (Romans 10:17).

When a group of people gathers to worship, and the most important and necessary thing going on there is listening, there's a need for *order*. The Holy Spirit led the apostle Paul to this important point when Paul saw how the congregation in Corinth was worshiping. After describing some disorderly practices in that congregation, Paul writes: "God is not a God of disorder but of peace" (1 Corinthians 14:33), and "Everything should be done in a fitting and orderly way" (1 Corinthians 14:40).

It's a little ironic that something created by the Holy Spirit with no rules attached to it should have to be put in order. But we worship in an orderly way out of love for our fellow worshipers. We want them to be able to listen to God rather than having their attention drawn to us.

Pentecost

When Lutherans come to worship in the summer, they see green cloths called paraments hanging on the altar. Most Lutheran pastors wear a stole that matches those cloths. All of that green color signals to the Lutheran worshiper that we are in the season of *Pentecost*.

Every year the Lutheran church takes half a year to review the entire life of Jesus. The other half of the year is called the Pentecost season, the time when we remember Jesus sending his Holy Spirit into our hearts through his Word and sacraments. The Holy Spirit causes us to grow in our faith, so we use green, the color of growing plants, to remind us of that spiritual progress.

The Pentecost season begins with the Sunday on which we remember Jesus sending his Holy Spirit in a special way on his disciples, to remind them of everything he told them and to make them reliable when they wrote down the New Testament for us. On that special Sunday, we remember what appeared as tongues of fire on the disciples' heads, and we use fiery red paraments and stoles.

That Sunday is called Pentecost because it takes place 50 days after Easter. It was a harvest festival in the Old Testament. Now it is the time in which we remember God's harvest of souls for his kingdom.

Some Lutherans refer to the last four Sundays of the Pentecost season as "End Times," when they recall Jesus' promise to return visibly at the end of the world. Paraments during that time are red (for the fire of judgment) and then white (for the holiness of Jesus, given to us to keep us safe at judgment day).

The four Sundays before Christmas are called Advent Sundays. *Advent* comes from a Latin word that means "arrival." Lutherans begin their review of the life of Jesus by remembering the thousands of years of believers waiting for God to fulfill his promise of the Savior. Since those waiting looked heavenward for the coming Savior, some Lutheran churches use sky blue paraments for Advent. Other Lutheran churches remember that the proper way to wait for God is with a penitent heart, so they use purple paraments that recall the suffering we caused Jesus when he was mocked by being dressed in a purple robe.

During the season of Advent, many Lutheran churches display a wreath of four or five candles. Lighting one more candle each Sunday reminds us how the promises of God shined brighter and brighter in the darkness as the day grew closer to the birth of the Savior. In some Lutheran churches, a pink candle on the third Sunday represents joy. A white candle in the middle of the wreath is called the Christ candle.

Most Lutherans celebrate Christmas on December 25th, although we don't know the exact date of Christ's birth. Then the paraments are white to remember the only birth in world history of a child free from sin.

The 12 days of Christmas last until January 6th. Some Christian churches celebrate that as the date of Christ's birth. Most Lutheran churches celebrate the visit of the wise men on that date, although the wise men visited the child more than 12 days after Jesus' birth.

The season of weeks following Christmas is called *Epiphany*, from a Greek word that means "reveal." During that time we remember how Jesus grew up and was revealed to the world as the Son of God. Green paraments recall his growth and the growth in faith of those who came to know him as their Savior.

Q
Quadragesima

After the season of Epiphany, the *Quadragesima* (from a Latin word that means "forty") days before Easter are called the Lenten season. Celebrated as the days *leng*then, it was originally the time before Easter when adults studied the Bible in order to become members of the church. Its 40 days are six full weeks, not counting Sundays, so the season begins on a Wednesday, commonly called Ash Wednesday.

Lent is a time when we review the suffering and death of Jesus, so the paraments are black (for sin) and purple (for repentance). The ashes on Ash Wednesday come from the practice of putting ashes on the forehead to say publicly that a person was sorry for sinning. The idea was that you were so sorry and humble that you had your forehead on the ground in the dust when you said so.

The Lenten season is followed by Easter, the most important festival of the year. It was originally called Pascha, (from a Greek word that means "Passover"). Jesus rose from the dead during the celebration of the Passover, a remembrance of when God spared his people who had the blood of a lamb on their doorposts in Egypt. Now God spares us because we have the blood of the Lamb of God covering all of our sin. Because we are washed clean by that blood, the paraments for Easter are white.

The Pascha festival acquired the name Easter in Northern Europe when pagan tribes converted to Christianity and celebrated the festival at a time when they had formerly worshiped the goddess of spring, Eostre. People who are bothered by the origin of the modern English name like to call it the Festival of the Resurrection of our Lord.

Reformation

A *reformation* of the Christian church happened in the 1500s when people realized that some of what the Roman Catholic church was teaching had been added to the Bible and was even against the Bible. People who studied the Bible realized that since the 600s, the church had accumulated a lot of false and confusing doctrine.

A German man named Martin Luther (1483–1546) published a revised liturgy in Latin in 1523. Three years later, in 1526, he published a service in German. Although it was not the first service published in the German language, it quickly became the most popular.

What principles did Martin Luther use to revise a liturgy that the Christian church had used for 1,000 years? After studying the Bible, he decided to look at every part of the service and keep whatever did not contradict the Bible. He rejected all false teachings and recommended adopting new practices only when they emphasized the gospel.

One of Luther's new practices was actually just restoring the old practice of participation of the congregation in worship. In his Latin service, he said that the hymns should be sung and the sermon should be preached in the language of the people (German). Therefore, in his German service, he replaced the traditional Latin songs with German hymns based on biblical texts. The people could hear and respond to the gospel in their own language even if they did not understand Latin.

Martin Luther offered his liturgies for other people to use, but he did not insist that people use them. Lutherans do not teach that everyone has to use exactly the same liturgy. Instead, Lutherans say in their Confessions, "Just as the dissimilar length of day and night does not injure the unity of the

Church, so we believe that the true unity of the Church is not injured by dissimilar rites instituted by men" (Apology of the Augsburg Confession, Articles 7 and 8, paragraph 33).

Sunday

God told the Old Testament believers to worship on Saturday. He called that day the Sabbath (a Hebrew word that means "rest") day, because it was on that day that God rested from creating the world. The New Testament believers worshiped on *Sunday*, which they called the Lord's Day. When did the day of worship switch?

The simple answer is that it switched to the day that Jesus rose from the dead, which was a Sunday. The resurrection is the difference between Christianity and all other religions. Every other religious leader dies and remains dead. But Christ rose from the dead and remains alive. To remember this central event, Christians gather for worship every Sunday.

But God did not command the New Testament believers to worship on Sunday. He did not say that Sunday was the new Sabbath Day. Instead, in the freedom of the gospel, God had the apostle Paul write: "Do not let anyone judge you by what you eat or drink, or with regard to a religious festival, a New Moon celebration or a Sabbath day. These are a shadow of the things that were to come; the reality, however, is found in Christ" (Colossians 2:16,17).

Jesus fulfilled the Old Testament Sabbath law by becoming our rest. We rest in the security of knowing that our sins are forgiven through him. And we look forward to a perfect rest in heaven.

Christians may worship on any day of the week. But most Lutheran churches choose to worship on Sunday in order to remember the resurrection of Jesus.

T
tradition

Some people like *traditions*. Some people don't like them. What does God have to say about them?

God is very clear that when traditions go against the Bible, they're sinful. He says: "You nullify the word of God for the sake of your tradition. . . . They worship me in vain; their teachings are but rules taught by men" (Matthew 15:6,9).

Whenever traditions in worship are valued over the Word of God, whenever they contradict the Word of God, whenever they threaten to cloud the Word of God in any way—then the traditions have to be thrown out as something God hates. Martin Luther wrote about his German service, "This or any other order shall be so used that whenever it becomes an abuse, it shall be straightway abolished and replaced by another" (*Luther's Works*, American Edition, Volume 53, page 90).

When a tradition helps speak or teach the Word of God, however, it is something God-pleasing. "This is what the Lord says: 'Stand at the crossroads and look; ask for the ancient paths, ask where the good way is, and walk in it, and you will find rest for your souls'" (Jeremiah 6:16).

The Lutheran church sees that one value of using traditional liturgies is that we do not have to follow a single person's whim, no matter how well-educated and godly that person may be, in planning how we are going to worship. Rather, we draw from thousands of years of experience, from millions of Christians who have gone before us, keeping what is good and eliminating the bad, all based on the Word of God.

eulogy

When a person dies, the body decays. The souls of believers go directly to heaven; the souls of unbelievers go directly to hell. The Bible is clear on these matters.

So why do Lutheran congregations have funerals? They certainly don't change what has happened to the soul or body of the person who died. Is it so that we can remember all of the good things a person did? That's what a *eulogy* (from a Greek word that means "compliment") is for, but many Lutheran churches do not even have eulogies connected to their funeral services. Why have funerals at all?

The simple answer is that funerals are for the living. Those still alive need to be reassured of the promises of God for the one who has died. They need to hear that God has promised peace to the person who died trusting in Jesus as their Savior. The funeral service is an opportunity to speak the gospel to people who have believed it for all of their lives and also to people who may never have heard it before.

But what if the person who died did not make a clear confession of faith in Jesus as Savior? While we do not conduct our normal Christian funeral service in that case, the Bible does not have rules about what Christian pastors and congregations may do to help the living. Some Lutheran churches have memorial, rather than funeral, services, in which they speak the gospel without promising that the person who died is in heaven. More often, a Lutheran pastor will counsel with the relatives of the person who died and speak clear gospel to them individually.

Death is not pretty. Nothing we do with the body will disguise the truth that death is the result of sin, and sin is not pretty either. But we know that Jesus has won the victory over death, proving that by rising from the dead. A Christian funeral service, with or without a eulogy, is an opportunity to comfort bereaved family and friends and to confess the promise of the resurrection of the dead in Christ.

VOWS

Most Lutheran churches have chosen a time at the end of elementary school and the beginning of high school when they encourage students to study the truths of the Bible more intensively. We call this confirmation (from a Latin word that means "make strong"). Lutherans teach the truths of the Bible to these students using the format of Luther's Small Catechism, a book that arranges Scripture passages by topic.

Martin Luther intended his catechism to help parents teach their children the truths of God's Word, particularly the gospel. Some Lutheran parents are actively involved in that teaching. Others allow teachers in the church to do most of the direct instruction.

After a period of years, Lutheran churches ask the students who have had confirmation instruction if they are ready to make a public confession that, as far as they have learned, the Lutheran church teaches just what the Bible teaches, no more and no less. The students then make a confession that their faith is the same as the faith of every other Lutheran Christian who has studied what the Lutheran church teaches from the Bible. Lutheran confirmands also *vow* to remain faithful to what God says in his Word until death. Some Lutherans also use the word *confirmation* for the exact day that the students take this vow in worship.

The Bible instructs both parents and church leaders to teach the Word of God faithfully. It does not set a time for confirmation, but it does promise that whenever we study the Word of God, it confirms us, that is, it makes us stronger in our faith.

It is wise never to give up a lifelong study of the Word of God, even after times of intensive study.

weddings

Marriage is one man and one woman, both truly single in the eyes of God, promising to live together for life. Why have a *wedding*? Marriage is also a civil ceremony in which two people change their legal status in the eyes of the state in a very specific way. But why have a wedding?

The answer is not for sentimental reasons, although most little girls and even some little boys dream of how their weddings should go. The reason Lutherans have weddings is not even to make the public announcement that the couple is living together with the blessing of God and not in sin, although that's a pretty good by-product of the ceremony.

The reason Lutherans have a wedding service is to worship Jesus Christ. Sometimes it's hard to tell that by looking at all of the outward trappings, which tend to draw attention to the bridal party and particularly to the bride. But a good Lutheran wedding service makes every effort to put the attention on all of the promises God makes to bless Christian couples and Christian households.

A Lutheran wedding will be like any other good worship: God comes to us in his Word, and we respond with praise and service. The music will draw attention to the Lord, not to the musicians or the bridal party. The parts spoken by the bride and groom will express confidence in the Lord's promises.

A Christian wedding service celebrates God's gracious gift of marriage. The congregation shares the joy of the bride and groom as they publicly promise lifelong love and faithfulness to each other.

your name

In the days when there were many adults who did not know how to read and write, it was okay for a person to sign a legal document with an X in the space where the person's name would go. Another person, preferably one able to read the document, would testify that the person who signed "X" was really carrying out the legal agreement the way it was written.

At your baptism, God set up a legal relationship with you. He made you his child. Even if you were very small and unable to sign your name, God promised that you had a clean conscience toward him through faith in Jesus. When he brought you to faith, he signed your "X" for you on the dotted line. Then, since you were a member of God's family, he gave you the family name: Father, Son, and Holy Spirit. Every time worship begins with that name, you are reminded that you are a member of God's family.

In Lutheran worship we admit that we are sinful members of God's perfect family and that we do not deserve to be adopted by our perfect Savior. Our names, our reputations, are dirtied by our thoughts and our words and our deeds. But God comes to us in his Word and restores our good names. He takes away our sin and gives us his righteousness, so that we can claim the family name of Jesus again in good faith.

It's important to stress the name of Jesus in our worship. Regardless of how important we think our own names are, in worship we grow less important and Jesus grows more important. His is the name above all names. Worship is a little taste of the joy of judgment day, when at the name of Jesus, every knee will bow in heaven and on earth and under the earth, and every tongue will confess that Jesus Christ is Lord, to the glory of God the Father.

X is the first letter in the Greek word for Christ. It is also the first letter of the Greek word for Christian. Let every part of worship be a reminder that your true identity is in Christ.

Y

your role in worship

Your role in worship is threatened.

It's threatened by the world, which wants to take you away from worship and toward self-indulgence. "You don't need to spend unproductive time in a place where you don't understand everything," it says. "There are a lot better ways to use your time. You could be getting more rest. You could be getting more exercise. You just need time for youself."

Your role in worship is threatened by the devil, who wants you to believe that you could never be a part of such a wonderful thing as worship. "You don't deserve to be here among these good people," he lies. "You don't really fit in, your kids will bother them, and besides, most of this music and sermon stuff is beyond you. You've gotten by just fine in life without a lot of this. Why set yourself up now to be disappointed?"

Your role in worship is threatened by your own sinful flesh, which wants to put the emphasis on your own comfort. "This doesn't quite feel right," it says. "It isn't my style, and it's not quite what I'm looking for. I need a little more entertainment. I want all of my needs met right away. I want to feel good, and this isn't always doing it for me."

Your real role in worship is passive. It's listening to the Word of God. It's receiving the gifts of forgiveness of sins, life, and salvation from God as he comes to you in Word and Sacrament. But it's also active. It's applying the Word of God to your life. It's the joyful response of the Holy Spirit in your heart as you sing and concentrate and pray.

Your real role in worship includes the encouragement of your fellow worshipers as you are worshiping, the love of your fellow worshipers as you experience the love of Christ, and the forgiveness of your fellow worshipers as you become aware of their shortcomings and sins, even as they and the Lord are forgiving you.

Z
Omega

One of the great hymns of the Old Testament is Psalm 119. Each verse of the psalm begins with a different letter of the Hebrew alphabet. In each verse the psalmist speaks about how wonderful the Word of God is. It's as if the inspired writer is worshiping God from *Aleph* to *Taw*, from *A* to *Z*.

One of the great hymns of the New Testament era is titled "Now Praise We Christ, the Holy One." In its original Latin, each verse of the hymn begins with a different letter of the Latin alphabet. It's a hymn of praise, glorifying God for events in the life of Jesus. It's as if the writer wants to worship God from *A* to *Z*.

In the Bible's great book of hymns, Revelation, Jesus claims the beginning and the end of the alphabet for himself. He says, "I am the Alpha and the *Omega*, the First and the Last, the Beginning and the End" (Revelation 22:13).

When Jesus—who was, and who is, and who is to come—is the beginning and the middle and the end of our Lutheran worship, then our focus is where God intends.

> "Of the Father's love begotten
> Ere the worlds began to be,
> He is Alpha and Omega,
> He the source, the ending he,
> Of the things that are, that have been,
> And that future years shall see
> Evermore and evermore." (CW 35:1)